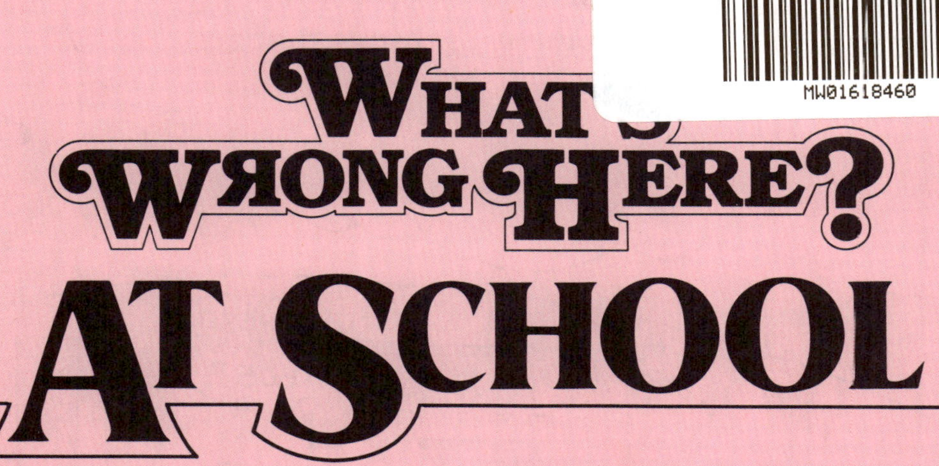

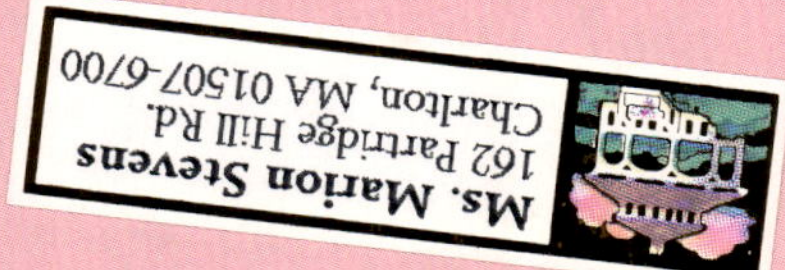

By

Tony Tallarico

7004 N. California Ave.
Chicago, IL. 60645

Manufactured in the United States of America

ANSWERS ON LAST PAGE

Monday morning. A new week of school begins with an enjoyable bus ride through town. Before the students arrive at school, can you find at least 13 things that are wrong with this picture?

IS IT MONDAY ALREADY?
WE HAVE A NEW STUDENT BUS DRIVER!
OOPS! I JUST LOST MY HOME-WORK PAPERS!
I FORGOT MY LUNCH!
I'M HUNGRY!
WAIT FOR ME!
THIS IS BETTER THAN A ROLLER COASTER!
I THINK I'M LOST!
I'M TAKING A SHORTCUT!
STUFF-IS-US!
STOP
HONK!
HONK!
KEEP YOUR EYE ON THE BALL!
OOOPS!
IT'S MOBY DICK!
I DON'T REMEMBER PASSING THIS WAY BEFORE!
?
NO
ISHING

Classes are about to start. Right before the bell rings, "It" sees 15 wrong things in the schoolyard. Do you?

I'M SHOW!
I'M TELL!
LAST STOP!
I BROUGHT "IT" LAST YEAR!
DOES HE WANT MY COOKIE?
I BROUGHT "IT" FOR SHOW AND TELL!
YIPES! I FORGOT TO BRING MINE!
UGH! I'M SUPPOSED TO PLAY THIS TUBA WHILE MARCHING !?!
CAN "IT" PLAY BASKETBALL?
?
I'M GOING OUT FOR THE BASKETBALL TEAM AS SOON AS I'M 4 FEET TALL!
COACH
DOES "IT" HAVE A HALL PASS?
I'M TRYING OUT FOR THE TRACK TEAM!

The first lesson of the day is Arithmetic. But, what's wrong here? Search for and find at least 12 things that are wrong in this classroom.

A
B
C
D
E
F
G
H
7
+8
16
7
+8
15
7
+8
17
ONE OF YOU IS CORRECT!

Special school programs are always interesting and a lot of fun. But there are at least 20 things wrong with this assembly. Can you find them?
GOOD MORNING STUDENTS! WE HAVE VERY INTERESTING GUESTS TODAY!
CHIRP!
DOES ANY-ONE HAVE A COLORING BOOK?
I WANT TO BE AN ARTIST!
I'M LOST!
HOW LONG WILL THIS TAKE?
INTO LUNCH TIME!
WHICH ONE IS THE ASTRONAUT?
Z-Z-Z-Z-Z!
I'M A JUNIOR!
I'M A SENIOR!
I'VE SEEN HIM ON TV!
ON THE NEWS?
NO! ON THE CARTOONS.
I DON'T BELIEVE I LEFT ANY-THING OUT!
HAS THE PROGRAM STARTED?
HURRY!
WHERE DO I SIT?

HURRY UP WITH THE INTRODUCTIONS, I'M GOING ON A SAFARI!
I'M DUE ON MARS IN 2 MINUTES!
HOW'S THE WEATHER DOWN THERE?
I HAVE A TICKET FOR YOU FOR DOUBLE PARKING.
IS THERE A PATIENT IN THE HOUSE?
MY SHIP CAME IN!!
SPECIAL POGRAM TODAY
I WANT TO BE AN ASTRONAUT!
I WANT TO BE A SINGER.
WAIT FOR ME!
I'M HUNGRY!
WHAT DID YOU BRING FOR LUNCH?
PEANUT BUTTER AND JELLY!
NO! I DON'T HAVE A CARROT!
OINK!
AHOY!
I'M A LATE KNIGHT!
I'M COMING!

The annual school play is scheduled to begin in a few days. However, there are a few things wrong with this full-dress rehearsal. Look for exactly <u>ten</u> of them.

"ALAS, POOR YORICK! I KNEW HIM"... BUT I DON'T KNOW MY LINES!
I LIKE THIS PROP!
I LIKE HAMLET!
I LIKE HAM AND EGGS!
I DON'T LIKE THE COLORS!
IT'S NOT REALISTIC.
I'M IN THE WRONG SHOW!
TO YELLOW BRICK ROAD
THE PLAY NEEDS MORE REHEARSAL!

The Arts and Crafts Club is meeting in room 221. Everything is under control...or is it? Find at least 12 things that are out of control and wrong with this picture.

YOU MADE MY NOSE TOO BIG!
I THINK ONE SLEEVE IS TOO LONG!
MY ROBOT WORKS!
ROOM 222
WILL IT FLY?
THIS IS THE WAY TO DO IT!
I AM HUNGRY!
I-I'M-D-DIZZ-D-DIZZY!
SMILE.
IT'S FOR THE BIRDS!
PINE CONES

Lunchtime! The students can't wait to dig into all that great food! Seek and find at least 13 things that are wrong in this lunchroom.

EXIT ONLY
SCHOOL LUNCH MENUE
FRESH FISH
TRY ME!
HOT DOG
MYSTERY PIZZA
?
by DUMBINO
BEANS
SNACK!
I'LL HAVE ONE OF THESE!
HOLD MY PLACE IN LINE. I'LL BE RIGHT BACK!
FILL IT UP!
NEXT!
WHAT'S FOR DESSERT?
MAKE MY DAY!
COME ON JOEY! I'LL SAVE YOU A SEAT!
I HAD A PERFECT SCORE ON THE EXAM!
WHAT? A ZERO?
RESERVED
DID I TAKE ENOUGH?
YUM... GOOD!
?
YOU ACTUALLY SPOKE TO FRANKIE?
YES, I DID!
HE'S SO CUTE!
CAN I SIT HERE?
YOU SURE CAN!

Today is the day of the big test. Exams aren't really that difficult if you study for them. If you don't, you'll have many wrong answers. Can you find 12 things that are wrong here?
QUIET, EVERYONE!
THIS IS SIMPLE!
THIS IS THE PITS!
THIS IS AWFUL!
I STUDIED. HERE I GO!
I'LL JUST CHECK THIS OVER.
HOW CAN SHE HAVE FINISHED? I HAVEN'T EVEN STARTED!
BAA!
FINISHED!
16 +37 53
16 +37 54
I QUIT!
Z-Z-Z-Z!!
I CAN'T BELIEVE I FINISHED THE WHOLE THING!
I KNOW THE ANSWER TO THIS ONE!
THIS IS DOOMS-DAY!
I'M HUNGRY!

I WANT TO GO HOME!
THIS IS NOT TOO BAD!
BRAINS, DO YOUR THING!
I COMPLETED THE EXAM!
FASTER-FASTER!
THIS IS NOT THAT HARD.
I CAN DO IT... I CAN DO IT... I *DID* IT!
ALL DONE!
I SHOULD HAVE STUDIED!
I SHOULD HAVE STAYED IN KINDERGARTEN!
WE SHOULD NOT HAVE EXAMS!
THIS IS A SNAP!
?
I LOST MY APPETITE!
HMMM.. 77 PLUS 10 EQUALS 90?
BRING ON MORE EXAMS!
I WISH IT WAS TOMORROW!
BLANK!

Gym is most students' favorite class. Mixed in with all the exercise, sports, and games are at least 18 wrong things for you to find. Go to it!
WHERE DID HE GO?
Z
WHERE DO YOU WANT THIS?
IT'S A GOOD VIEW FROM UP HERE!
AM I RUNNING IN THE RIGHT DIRECTION?
7
VERY GOOD CLASS!
HERE I COME, READY OR NOT!
FEET DO YOUR THING!
MY FEET ARE TOO FAR AWAY!
HERE'S MY FIRST PITCH!
PLAY BALL!
UMPIRE

RUN!
RUN!
PUFF!
THIS IS SIMPLE!
GRUNT!
MOVE IT!
I'M NEXT!
HURRY UP AND SHOOT!
WE ARE IN THIS ISSUE!
I CAN'T DO THAT!
OK! EVERYONE JOG!
SPORTS ILL-STATED
THINGS LOOK DIFFERENT!
15-16-17-18-21-22-24-25-27-
THIS COULD BE THE START OF MY CAREER!
FIRE AWAY!

This year the class trip is to Prehistoric Times Amusement Park. The Dinosaur Slide looks like fun! Find at least 15 things wrong with this picture.

STEP RIGHT UP, KIDS. NO PUSHING!
I'M NEXT!
IT'S NIGHT-TIME!
THIS IS WILD!
THIS WAY ONYL
ONE WAY
SPACE FOUR RENT!
STEP RIGHT UP, KIDS. NO PUSHING!
CAN I HAVE YOUR AUTOGRAPH?
TICKKETS
THAT WAS FUN!
LET'S DO IT AGAIN!
PARK OPENS 9 AM
DUNNOSAUR SLIDE
?
DO YOU LIKE THIS, FRED?
I SURE DO, BARNEY!

Another week of school has ended. Some students are staying for after-school activities. Before the rest leave for home, there are at least 18 wrong things here for you to find.

WHICH WAY DO I GO?
I CAN WALK HOME!
UNGH! PUFF!!
I HOPE THE BUS DRIVER KNOWS THE WAY HOME TODAY!
THIS IS NOT GOING TO WORK!
YOU'RE DOING A GOOD JOB, JOHNNY!
STOP
I BEARLY PASSED THE EXAM!
YOU LOOK CUTE N YOUR NIFORM.
I GOT 100 IN MATH!
THAT'S GREAT!
WE'LL SEE YOU AGAIN!
BYE!

ANSWERS